PSYCHIATRIC AND PSYCHOLOGICAL EVIDENCE

1987 Supplement
Current through May 31, 1987

Daniel W. Shuman
Professor of Law
School of Law
Southern Methodist University
Dallas, Texas

*Insert in the pocket at the
back of the bound volume.*

SHEPARD'S/McGRAW-HILL, INC.
P.O. Box 1235
Colorado Springs, CO 80901

D0005013

Bound Book ISBN 0-07-057179-1
Supplement ISBN 0-07-172125-8

2 Psychiatric and Psychological Diagnosis

§2.02 Diagnostic Categories: DSM-III

Page 22, add at end of section:

In 1987 a revision of DSM-III, DSM-III-R, was published. *Diagnostic and Statistical Manual of Mental Disorders* (3d ed rev 1987). The revision maintains the same basic multiaxial structure but attempts to incorporate new studies inconsistent with some diagnostic criteria and to resolve diagnostic inconsistencies and contradictions. One specific feature of DSM-III-R of note is the Cautionary Statement, which states in part:

> The purpose of DSM-III-R is to provide clear descriptions of diagnostic categories in order to enable clinicians and investigators to diagnose, communicate about, study, and treat the various mental disorders. It is to be understood that inclusion here, for clinical and research purposes, of a diagnostic category such as Pathological Gambling or Pedophilia does not imply that the condition meets legal or other nonmedical criteria for what constitutes mental disease, mental disorder, or mental disability. The clinical and scientific considerations involved in categorization of these conditions as mental disorders may not be wholly relevant to legal judgments, for example, that take into account such issues as individual responsibility, disability determination, and incompetency.

DSM-III-R at xxix.

This approach, which attempts to avoid making legally relevant conclusions in the context of a diagnostic system designed for the use of clinicians and investigators, has not always been reflected in the use of DSM-III in the judicial context. For example, the regulations implementing the Social Security Disability Benefits Reform Act of 1984 are designed to bring the disability criteria in closer harmony with DSM-III. (Final regulations have been published at 50 Fed Reg 35,038 (1985) and will be codified at 20 CFR 404, subt P, App 61.) In the context of a state requirement of objective medical evidence of a psychiatric disability for workers compensation claims, the Supreme Court of New Jersey held that DSM-III, while not a panacea for this problem, provides a framework for "demonstrable objective medical evidence as the profession of psychiatry conceives it." *Saunderlin v EI DuPont Co*, 102 NJ 402, 508 A2d 1095, 1101 (1986). Similarly, in *State v Huntley*, 302 Or 418, 730 P2d 1234 (1986), a criminal sentencing procedure in which the critical question was whether the defendant suffered from a severe personality disorder, the psychiatrist, prosecutor, and defense attorney all utilized DSM-III and the appellate court suggested that the trial court could utilize the diagnostic criteria for antisocial personality disorder set forth there in rejecting the psychiatrist's conclusions. In other instances, however, courts have been unwilling to be limited by DSM-III. For example, in *People v Lang*, 113 Ill 2d 407, 498 NE2d 1105 (1986), the court ruled that mental illness, for purposes of civil commitment, was not restricted to the diagnostic classifications set forth in DSM III.

§2.03   —Multiaxial Diagnosis

Page 24, add at end of section:

DSM-III-R maintains the same multaxial diagnostic approach. However, the axes have in some instances been modified. The DSM-III-R axes are as follows:

> Axis I: Clinical Syndromes and V Codes (no change from DSM-III) (DSM-III-R at 16)
>
> Axis II: Developmental Disorders and Personality Disorders (change from DSM-III to include mental retardation, specific developmental disorders, and pervasive developmental disorders as Developmental Disorders in Axis II) (DSM-III-R at 16)
>
> Axis III: Physical Disorders and Conditions (no change from DSM-III) (DSM-III-R at 18)
>
> Axis IV: Severity of Psychosocial Stressors (change in rating of stressors from DSM-III with attempt to categorize coded events as either acute events or enduring circumstances and elimination of coding for minimal level stressors) (DSM-III-R at 18-20)
>
> Axis V: Highest Level of Adaptive Functioning (inclusion of new scale for psychological functioning, as well as social and occupa-

tional functioning previously included in DSM-III) (DSM-III-R at 20)

§2.04 —Hierarchy of Disorders

Page 24, add after first paragraph of section:

One change in DSM-III-R is the elimination of certain restrictions imposed by DSM-III's approach to diagnostic hierarchies that did not permit giving multiple diagnoses when the occurrence of different syndromes was present in a single episode of an illness, because of the theoretical approach that disorders higher in the hierarchy might present symptoms found lower in the hierarchy but not vice versa. The change in DSM-III-R is set forth in two principles:

1. When an Organic Mental Disorder can account for the symptoms, it preempts the diagnosis of any other disorder that could produce the same symptoms (e.g., Organic Anxiety Disorder preempts Panic Disorder).

2. When a more pervasive disorder, such as Schizophrenia, commonly has associated symptoms that are the defining symptoms of a less pervasive disorder, it is diagnosed if both its defining symptoms and associated symptoms are present. For example, only Schizophrenia (not Schizophrenia and Dysthemia) should be diagnosed when the defining symptoms of Schizophrenia are present along with chronic mild depression (which is a common associated symptom of Schizophrenia).

DSM-III-R at xxiv-xxv.

§2.07 —Schizophrenic Disorders

Page 33, text, add after Item F:

DSM-III-R has simplified the diagnostic criteria for what is now called Schizophrenia rather than Schizophrenic Disorders. Some of the changes include elimination of the requirement that the illness begin before age 45 and the addition of a requirement that the symptoms described in subpart A be present for one week at minimum. DSM-III-R at 194-95.

§2.08 —Organic Mental Disorders

Page 33, text, add after first paragraph of section:

DSM-III-R has added a category for Posthallucinogenic Disorder for use in cases of repeated "flashbacks" after the use of hallucinogenic drugs. DSM-III-R at 147-48.

§2.09 —Affective Disorders

Page 35, text, add after first paragraph of section:

DSM-III-R has renamed this group of disorders as Mood Disorders. The grouping of disorders has been changed to group together Bipolar Disorders and Depressive Disorders. DSM-III-R at 213.

§2.17 —Personality Tests

Page 56, add to note 124:

West v Martin, 11 Kan App 2d 55, 713 P2d 957 (1986) (computer score and evaluation of MMPI by orthopedic surgeon is hearsay and does not qualify under business records exception as record of physician, but if at all, as record of testing service; thus, physician not proper foundation witness).

3   Treatment

§3.16 —Limitations

Page 89, add to note 98:

Martin & Peter, *Civil Commitment and Consent for Electroconvulsive Therapy in Ontario,* 32 Can J Psychiatry 35 (1987); Mahler & Dinwiddie, *Studies in Involuntary Civil Commitment and Involuntary Electroconvulsive Therapy,* 174 J Nervous & Mental Disorders 97 (1986).

Page 89, add at end of section:

The use of ECT has decreased but has not disappeared. See Thompson & Blaine, *Use of ECT in the United States in 1975 and 1980,* 144 Am J Psychiatry 557 (1987); Mahler & Dinwiddie, *Studies in Involuntary Civil Commitment and Involuntary Electroconvulsive Therapy,* 174 J Nervous & Mental Disorders 97 (1987).

§3.19 —Limitations

Page 91, add to note 104:

E. Valenstein, Great and Desperate Cures: The Rise and Decline of Psychosurgery and Other Radical Treatments for Mental Illness (1986).

6

Obtaining Psychiatric and Psychological Evidence

§6.02 The Fallacy of the Impartial Expert

Page 140, add to note 1:

For an interesting historical perspective on this question, see King, *Medicine 100 Years Ago: The Doctor and the Law*, 257 J Am Med Assn 2204 (1987). See also Kennedy, Kelley, & Homat, *A Test of the "Hired Gun" Hypothesis in Psychiatric Testimony*, 57 Psychology Rep 117 (1985).

§6.18 —Civil

Page 160, add to note 57:

But see West v Martin, 11 Kan App 2d 55, 713 P2d 957 (1986) (trial court abused its discretion in failing to permit physician to testify as an expert who was not named on interrogatory or in witness list, in absence of showing that plaintiff attempted to mislead defendant or that defendant had been misled).

Page 160, add to note 62:

Note, *Discovery of the Non-Testifying Expert Witness' Identity Under FRCP: You Can't Tell the Players Without a Program*, 37 Hastings LJ 201 (1985).

§6.19 —Criminal

Page 163, add to note 72:

State v Duell, 332 SE2d 246 (W Va 1986) (state's failure to provide defendant with results of psychological tests conducted by the state's psychiatrist and properly requested by defendant was reversible error). *See also* United States v Buchbinder, 796 F2d 910 (7th Cir 1986) (trial

6

court did not abuse its discretion under Fed R Crim P 12.2 in denying defendant right to present expert testimony when defendant did not give timely notice of intention to present expert testimony regarding mental condition).

7

General Requirements for the Presentation of Expert Psychiatric and Psychological Evidence

§7.02 Required and Permitted Psychiatric and Psychological Evidence

Page 175, add to note 22:

United States v Buchbinder, 796 F2d 910 (7th Cir 1986) (no error to exclude expert testimony that defendant was so depressed as to be unable to form specific intent, where lay testimony supporting this conclusion was presented and prejudicial effect may have outweighed relevance). *But see* United States v McBride, 786 F2d 45 (2d Cir 1986) (error to exclude expert testimony by psychiatrist that defendant who did not raise insanity defense suffered from residual organic brain impairment rendering it less likely that she had culpable knowledge of criminal conduct involved).

Page 176, add to note 23:

State v Wyoming, 723 P2d 564 (Wyo 1986) (lay testimony may be sufficient response to defense psychiatrists to present question for jury of defendant's sanity).

§7.03 Validity of Psychiatric and Psychological Theory

Page 177, add to note 30:

See Note, *The Frye Doctrine and Relevancy Approach Controversy: An Empirical Evaluation,* 74 Geo LJ 1769 (1986).

Page 177, add to note 32:

United States v Shorter, 809 F2d 54 (DC Cir 1987) (trial court properly excluded expert testimony that defendant was compulsive gambler as defense to tax evasion, where there was no general acceptance in community of psychiatrists and psychologists that relationship existed between compulsive gambling and tax evasion); People v John W, 185 Cal App 3d 801, 229 Cal Rptr 783 (1986) (psychologist's testimony that defendant was not a sexual deviate based in part on penile plethysmograph did not meet standard for acceptance in scientific community); State v Hodges, 239 Kan 63, 716 P2d 563 (1986) (expert testimony on battered woman syndrome meets *Frye* test of general acceptance in relevant scientific community); State v Black, 46 Wash App 259, 730 P2d 698 (1986) (error to admit evidence of rape trauma syndrome in absence of evidence of acceptance in relevant scientific community).

§7.04   —Scientific Invalidity

Page 178, add to note 34:

Psychiatric Inst of Wash v Allen, 509 A2d 619 (DC Ct App 1986) (no error in failure to give jury instruction that psychiatry and psychology are not exact sciences).

Page 179, add to note 38:

Hedges, *How Hard is Hard Science, How Soft is Soft Science?*, 42 Am Psychologist 443 (1987).

§7.05   —Diagnostic Imprecision

Page 180, text, add after second full paragraph:

During 1987 a revision, DSM-III-R, was published, in part to address studies that revealed problems with DSM-III's diagnostic criteria. Thus it is now appropriate to focus the discussion about diagnostic precision on this revised system.

§7.06   —Predictive Limitations

Page 183, add to note 60:

In United States v Salerno, 55 USLW 4663 (US 1987), the Supreme Court upheld, against Fifth and Eight Amendment challenges, that portion of the Bail Reform Act of 1984 that permits pretrial detention of persons who would endanger the safety of the community, thereby sanctioning another context in which psychiatric and psychological predictions of future dangerousness may be offered.

8

Qualification of the Expert

§8.02   Psychiatrist Versus Psychologist

Page 190, add to note 10:

Kingsbury, *Cognitive Differences Between Clinical Psychologists and Psychiatrists,* 42 Am Psychologist 152 (1987).

Page 191, add to note 15:

Commonwealth v Monico, 396 Mass 793, 488 NE2d 1168 (1986) (qualification of psychologist as expert witness on question of criminal responsibility turns on actual experience rather than academic degrees); Lundgren v Eustermann, 370 NW2d 877 (Minn 1985) (psychologist with training and experience in pharmacology not qualified to testify to standard of care in malpractice action for physician in prescribing antipsychotic drugs); McDonnell v County of Nassau, 129 Misc 2d 228, 492 NYS2d 699 (1985) (psychologist who was never on staff at any hospital was not competent to testify in malpractice action against psychiatrist as to standard of psychiatric care in a general hospital); Howle v PYA/Monarch, Inc, 288 SC 586, 344 SE2d 157, 161 (Ct App 1986) ("psychologist, once qualified as an expert witness by reason of education, training, and experience, is competent to testify as to diagnosis, prognosis, and causation of mental and emotional disturbance").

§8.03   Physician versus Psychiatrist

Page 192, add to note 16:

Baxle v Indiana, 480 NE2d 561 (Ind 1985) (general physician, half of whose cases included patients with mental and emotional problems, was permitted to offer opinion as to defendant's mental state at the time of the offense).

Page 192, add to note 19:

Curry v Giant Food Co, 522 A2d 1283 (DC Ct App 1987) (exclusion of testimony of physician who had one year of psychiatric training 40 years ago, when offered on the issue of the foreseeability of acquiring an alcoholic habit following an arrest and forcible detention, was proper); State v Perry, 502 So 2d 543 (La 1986) (no error in trial court's giving greater weight to psychiatric diagnosis of psychiatrists than that of nonpsychiatrists); Turner v Regional Transit Auth, 498 So 2d 777 (La Ct App 1987) (award of future medical expenses for psychiatric care could not be sustained based solely on testimony of nonpsychiatric physician).

§8.06 —Licensing

Page 196, add to note 27:

Sutphin v Platt, 720 SW2d 455 (Tenn 1986) (requirement of state medical malpractice act that medical expert witness be licensed to practice in Tennessee or a contiguous state is constitutional).

§8.07 —Specialty Certification

Page 196, add to note 28:

See Reade & Ratzan, *Yellow Professionalism: Advertising by Physicians in the Yellow Pages,* 316 New Eng J Med 1315 (1987) (12% of physicians studied who advertised in the yellow pages as specialists were not board certified).

Page 197, add to note 29:

Campbell v Pommier, 5 Conn App 29, 496 A2d 975 (1985) (board certification is not prerequisite to testimony as an expert).

9

Form and Mode of Presentation of Psychiatric and Psychological Evidence

§9.02   Basis for Opinion

Page 205, add to note 4:

Carlson, *Policing the Bases of Modern Expert Testimony*, 39 Vand L Rev 577 (1986).

§9.03   —Personal Knowledge

Page 207, add to note 11:

Oldsen v People, 732 P2d 1132 (Colo 1986) (child's statement to physician concerning abuse did not meet Rule 803(4) requirements where it was not shown that the child understood the need to provide accurate information for medical treatment).

§9.04   —Hypothetical Questions

Page 209, add to note 23:

Ashby v State, 486 NE2d 469 (Ind 1985) (psychiatrist who did not examine defendant did not need to be asked hypothetical question to elicit opinion on defendant's sanity).

Page 209, add to note 24:

Sharpe v South Carolina Dept of Mental Health, 354 SE2d 778 (SC Ct App 1987) (opinion by psychiatrist witness without firsthand knowledge of facts must be based on a hypothetical question).

Page 210, add to note 29:

McGrady v United States, 650 F Supp 379 (DSC 1986) (opinion of psychiatrist who did not examine deceased, sought to be introduced on the issue of deceased's dangerousness based on review of historical facts in medical file, was too speculative to be received in evidence).

§9.05 —Extrajudicial Sources

Page 211, add to note 38:

United States v Wright, 783 F2d 1091 (DC Cir 1986) (psychiatrist may reasonably rely, under Fed R Evid 703, on out-of-court statement of patient in reaching a diagnosis); Bender v State, 472 So 2d 1370 (Fla Dist Ct App 1985) (testifying psychiatrist may rely on unadmitted CAT scan); Clark v Clark, 220 Neb 771, 371 NW2d 749 (1985) (testifying psychiatrist may reasonably base opinion on records of previous treating psychiatrist); MED v JPM, 3 Va App 391, 350 SE2d 215 (1986) (psychologist could express opinion on visitation based on out-of-court statement of child).

Page 211, add to note 42:

But see State v Vinik, 398 NW2d 788 (Iowa 1987) (basis of opinion of psychologist, which included interviews with defendant's friends and neighbors, was not shown by the record to be information ordinarily or reasonably used by other psychologists).

Page 212, add to note 45:

United States v Wright, 783 F2d 1091 (DC Cir 1986) (information relied upon by expert under Fed R Evid 703 that is not independently admitted may come in under Fed R Evid 705 to permit jury to evaluate expert's reasoning, but not as substantive evidence); People v Lang, 113 Ill 2d 407, 498 NE2d 1105 (1986) (psychiatrist may disclose extrajudicial statement upon which opinion is based not for its truth but to explain the basis for the expert's opinion).

§9.07 —Degree of Certainty

Page 212, add to note 49:

Psychiatric Inst of Wash v Allen, 509 A2d 619 (DC Cir App 1986) (psychiatrist's testimony that if reasonable care had been rendered there was an excellent chance that the decedent would have lived met requirements of reasonable medical certainty); Commonwealth v Terry, 521 A2d 398, 404 (Pa 1987) (psychiatric testimony is not admissible "unless it speaks to more than a mere possibility"); Heald v State, 492 NE2d 671 (Ind 1986) (no abuse of discretion in trial court's requirement that expert's opinion on defendant's sanity satisfy standard of reasonable medical certainty).

§9.08 —Conclusions

Page 215, add to note 61:

United States v Hillsberg, 812 F2d 328 (7th Cir 1987) (Fed R Evid 704(b) prohibits a psychiatric opinion as to whether intoxication prohibited defendant from conforming his conduct to the requirements of the law); United States v Alexander, 805 F2d 1458 (11th Cir 1986) (Rule 704(b) does not violate ex post facto or equal protection clause of the federal constitution); United States v Freeman, 804 F2d 1574 (11th Cir 1986) (704(b) does not unconstitutionally limit the right to present a defense); United States v Windfelder, 790 F2d 576 (7th Cir 1986) (704(b) limitations not applicable to the mental state of someone other than the defendant or testimony of a witness not qualified on the workings of the human mind, here an IRS agent providing an opinion on taxpayer's intent to make a gift); United States v Prickett, 790 F2d 35 (6th Cir 1986) (704(b) does not violate ex post facto clause when applied to trial of act which occurred before rule's effective date); United States v Mest, 789 F2d 1069 (4th Cir 1986) (same); United States v Frisbee, 623 F Supp 1217, 1224 (D Cal 1985) (limitation of 704(b) permits experts to present only "diagnosis, the facts upon which their diagnoses are based, and the characteristics of any mental diseases or defects the experts believe the defendant possessed during the relevant time period").

Page 215, add to note 62:

People v Whitler, 171 Cal App 3d 337, 214 Cal Rptr 610 (1985) (§29 is constitutional); People v Sanders, 154 Cal App 3d 197, 201 Cal Rptr 411 (1984) (defense psychiatrist could state the effects of PCP generally and as to this witness, but not that as a result of PCP the defendant did not satisfy statutory intent or malice requirements); People v Jackson, 152 Cal App 3d 961, 199 Cal Rptr 848 (1984) (§29 does not deprive defendant of right to present a defense).

§9.09 —Psychobabble

Page 217, add to note 74:

Illinois Psychological Assn v Falk, 638 F Supp 876 (ND Ill 1986) (judges should require psychiatrists and psychologists to state and explain their conclusions in words understandable to laypersons).

§9.10 Mode of Presentation

Page 217, add to note 76:

Sangster v State, 70 Md App 456, 521 A2d 811 (1987) (written psychiatric report on competence to stand trial did not violate hearsay rule or confrontation clause).

Page 218, add to note 81:

Williams v McClain, 520 A2d 1374 (Pa 1987) (hospital record containing social worker's conclusions that patient's problems predated treatment were not admissible absent showing of expertise in fields of psychology or psychiatry).

10

General Limitations on Psychiatric and Psychological Evidence

§10.01 Introduction

Page 224, add to note 4:

Although disclosure of patient confidences by a therapist in a judicial setting is generally thought not to give rise to an actionable breach of privacy, voluntary disclosure by the therapist without legal compulsion may give rise to a claim for relief by the patient. Cutter v Brownbridge, 228 Cal Rptr 545 (Ct App 1986).

Page 224, add to note 5:

Quinn v Kent Gen Hosp, 617 F Supp 1226 (D Del 1985) (federal common law does not recognize a physician-patient privilege).

Page 224, add to note 6:

Calloway v Marvel, 110 FRD 45 (SDNY 1986) (court recognized claim of psychiatrist-patient privilege in the absence of formal federal rule creating a privilege).

§10.02 The Physician-Patient Privilege—General Rule

Page 226, add to note 16:

Robinson v Commonwealth, 399 Mass 131, 503 NE2d 31 (1987) (in manslaughter prosecution of mother for death of infant, mother's conversation with staff psychiatrist in waiting room following hospitalization of infant, initiated by the psychiatrist to address mother's feelings about her infant's condition, constituted treatment); State v Miller, 709 P2d 225 (Or 1985) (defendant's murder confession to telephone receptionist at state hospital in attempt to speak with a doctor was privileged). *But see* United States v Crews, 781 F2d 826 (10th Cir 1986) (threats against life of the president made by a voluntary psychiatric inpatient to a nurse were not privileged, because of absence of psychotherapist-patient privilege in Federal Rules of Evidence and also because defendant disclosed threats to the Secret Service following *Miranda* warnings); State v Irish, 391 NW2d 137 (Neb 1986) (statements made by patient to treating physician following an accident concerning drinking and loss of control of vehicle, not made in response to questions relevant to treatment or diagnosis, not privileged).

Page 227, add to note 18:

Simpson v Braider, 104 FRD 512 (DDC 1985) (physician-patient privilege as applied to mental health practitioners protects not only information communicated by parents of minor patient to psychiatrist, but also information concerning treatment communicated by psychiatrist to parents).

Page 228, add to note 21:

Note, *The Case for a Federal Psychotherapist-Patient Privilege That Protects Patient Identity*, 1985 Duke LJ 1217.

§10.03 —Waiver

Page 229, add to note 28:

Novak v Ratham, 106 Ill 2d 478, 478 NE2d 1334 (1985) (presentation of psychiatrist as defense witness in a criminal trial against the patient waived the privilege in a subsequent action against the psychiatrist for wrongful release of the patient and patient's subsequent killing of civil plaintiff's daughter).

Page 229, add to note 29:

Clark v Clark, 220 Neb 771, 371 NW2d 749 (1985) (filing petition for dissolution of marriage in which fitness to have custody of child was at issue waived physician-patient privilege); New Jersey v McBride, 517 A2d 152 (NJ Super Ct App Div 1986) (institution of criminal prosecution against husband for assault waived privilege as to diagnosis of plaintiff's mental condition alleged to result from defendant's conduct). *But see* Kansas v Munyon, 726 P2d 1333 (Kan 1986) (institution of criminal prosecution for sexual assault of child did not waive psychologist-patient privilege as to communications between psychologist, child, and child's mother, who was defendant's former wife).

Page 230, add to note 32:

In some jurisdictions an even more limited approach to waiver has been taken. For example, in State v Pierson, 201 Conn 211, 514 A2d 724 (1986), the Supreme Court of Connecticut held that the state's presentation of the testimony of a therapist, who had treated a child before and after an alleged sexual assault, to show the absence of any inconsistencies in the child's complaint did not impliedly waive the privilege as to treatment of the child generally. The court did rule, however, under the confrontation clause, that a more limited inquiry was required into the possibility that the therapist possessed information about the mental condition of the complainant that might be admissible for impeachment of the complainant.

Page 230, add to note 33:

Bain v Superior Court, 148 Ariz 331, 714 P2d 824 (1986) (medical malpractice action against surgeon for failure to discover that patient's symptoms were attributable to psychological factors did not waive psychologist-patient privilege for earlier counseling for marital problems); People v District Court, 719 P2d 722 (Colo 1986) (testimony in criminal proceeding by victim of sexual assault about specifics of assault did not waive psychologist-patient privilege for counseling sought by victim after the assault); Moore v Grandview Hosp, 25 Ohio St 3d 194, 495 NE2d 934 (1986) (medical malpractice action against hospital and physician who delivered child for negligence in birth of child did not waive privilege as to child's treating physician); State *ex rel* Klieger v Alby, 125 Wis 2d 468, 373 NW2d 57 (1985) (commencement of medical malpractice action for birth of child did not permit defense attorneys to interview nondefendant treating neonatologist without plaintiff's attorney present).

§10.04   —Exceptions

Page 231, text, add after first paragraph:

Unlike the attorney-client privilege, which typically recognizes an exception or exclusion for communications relating to the performance of future crimes, the rationale of the physician-patient privilege, particularly in the context of psychotherapy, may not result in a future crimes exception. *Mutual of Omaha Insurance Co v American National Bank & Trust Co,* 610 F Supp 546 (D Minn 1985).

Page 231, add to note 39:

Tex R Crim Evid 509.

Page 231, add to note 40:

In re LaBelle, 107 Wash 2d 196, 728 P2d 138 (1986). *But see In re* KS, 405 NW2d 78 (Wis 1987) (exception to physician-patient and psychologist-patient privilege applicable in involuntary hospitalization proceedings does not apply in guardianship or protective placement proceedings).

Page 231, add to note 43:

In Pennsylvania v Ritchie, 107 S Ct 989 (1987), the Supreme Court concluded that those portions of state files containing investigations of child abuse that reveal information favorable to the accused and that might reasonably affect the outcome of the case if admitted into evidence, must be turned over to the defendant. In a slightly different context, it has been held that reporting a suspected act of child abuse under the requirements of a child abuse reporting law was cloaked by a grant of absolute immunity from liability for making the report. Storch v Silverman, 213 Cal Rptr 27 (Ct App 1986).

§10.05 The Psychiatrist, Psychologist, and Psychotherapist-Patient Privileges

Page 235, add to note 68:

In re Grand Jury Subpoenas Duces Tecum Dated Jan 30, 1986, 638 F Supp 794 (D Me 1986) (psychotherapist-patient privilege does not prevent disclosure of patient names in response to grand jury subpoena directed to therapist's corporation); Commonwealth v Korbin, 395 Mass 284, 479 NE2d 674 (1985) (court would compel disclosure of patient names, appointments, fees, and diagnoses, but not substantive communications, in Medicaid fraud investigation of psychiatrist).

§10.07 —Civil Proceedings

Page 238, add to note 82:

Note, *Discovery of the Nontestifying Expert Witness' Identity Under the Federal Rules of Civil Procedure: You Can't Tell the Players Without a Program,* 37 Hastings LJ 201 (1985).

§10.08   —Criminal Proceedings

Page 240, add to note 92:

State v Anderson, 44 Wash App 644, 723 P2d 464 (1986) (raising insanity defense waives attorney-client privilege for communications between defendant and defense psychiatrist); State v Schneider, 402 NW2d 779 (Minn 1987) (prosecutor may call as a witness a psychiatrist who was retained by defense counsel to examine defendant but not called as a witness by defendant).

§10.09   Constitutional Support for the Psychotherapist-Patient Privilege

Page 242, add to note 103:

But see In re Search Warrant, 810 F2d 67 (3d Cir 1987) (seizure of patient records in insurance fraud investigation did not violate patients' right to privacy because of expected disclosures to insurers by patients and safeguards imposed in investigation).

§10.10   Federal Program Limitations

Page 245, add to note 110:

State v Friend, 385 NW2d 313 (Minn Ct App 1986) (federal program limitations protecting patient records does not preempt limited disclosure requirements of state's child sexual abuse law).

11   Criminal Proceedings: Pretrial

§11.01   Bail—The Legal Standard

Page 256, add to note 13:

Ewing, *Schall v Martin: Preventive Detention and Dangerousness Through the Looking Glass*, 34 Buffalo L Rev 173 (1985).

Page 257, add to note 15:

In United States v Salerno, 55 USLW 4663 (US 1987), the Supreme Court upheld, against Fifth and Eighth Amendment challenges, the constitutionality of that portion of the Bail Reform Act of 1984 that permitted pretrial detention of persons who would endanger the safety of the community.

§11.03   —Basis

Page 259, add to note 26:

United States v $100,000 in United States Currency, 602 F Supp 712 (SDNY 1985) (bail hearings do not normally permit time for pretrial discovery, and attendance by nonparty witnesses is rare).

§11.04   —Limitations

Page 261, add to note 36:

United States v Acevedo-Ramos, 755 F2d 203 (1st Cir 1985); United States v Gallo, 653 F Supp 320 (EDNY 1986); United States v DiVarco, 602 F Supp 1029 (ND Ill 1985).

§11.06   Competence to Stand Trial—The Legal Standard

Page 262, add to note 39:

Commonwealth v Barnes, 399 Mass 385, 504 NE2d 624 (1987) (finding that defendant was competent to stand trial permits inference that defendant is competent to waive counsel); New York v Kent, 507 NYS2d 353 (1986) (due process required that evaluation of defendant's fitness take place in extradition proceedings); State v Champagne, 497 A2d 1242 (NH 1985) (*Dusky* standard applies for purposes of all trial proceedings). *But see* Colorado v Connelly, 107 S Ct 515 (1986) (confession by mentally ill defendant obtained in the absence of police coercion does not violate limitations of Fifth or Fourteenth Amendment).

Page 262, add to note 43:

See generally Winick, *Restructuring Competency to Stand Trial*, 32 UCLA L Rev 921 (1985).

Page 262, add to note 46:

People v Lang, 113 Ill 2d 407, 498 NE2d 1105 (1986) (fact that a person is mentally ill and subject to civil commitment proceedings is not dispositive of fitness to stand trial); State v Perry, 502 So 2d 543 (La 1987) (defendant diagnosed alternately as having character disorder and schizophrenia not necessarily incompetent to stand trial).

Page 264, add to note 53:

United States v Vamos, 797 F2d 1146 (2d Cir 1986), *cert denied,* 55 USLW 3473 (US 1987) (where defendant did not engage in any unusual behavior during trial and defense counsel did not indicate grounds to question defendant's competence at trial, competency hearing not required).

§11.07   —The Role of the Expert

Page 264, add to note 55:

Merely because psychiatric or psychological testimony is received and is uncontradicted, it does not follow that courts or juries will always be compelled to accept the conclusions of the expert witnesses. *See, e.g.,* McFadden v United States, 814 F2d 144 (3d Cir 1987); State v Perkins, 518 A2d 715 (Me 1986). *But see* Meraz v State, 714 SW2d 108 (Tex Civ App 1986).

Page 265, add at end of section:

The existence of a mental disorder does not necessarily equate with incompetence to stand trial. A mental disorder must be functionally related to the ability to consult with counsel and assist in one's defense to render a defendant incompetent to stand trial. *United States v Vamos*, 797 F2d 1146 (2d Cir 1986), *cert denied*, 55 USLW 3473 (US 1987).

§11.08 —Basis

Page 265, add at end of section:

An additional source of information about the defendant's competence to stand trial may be the alleged victim, particularly when the victim's testimony constitutes evidence that the defendant indicated an awareness that charges would be brought for the act committed. *Brown v Georgia*, 349 SE2d 452 (Ga 1986).

§11.09 —Limitations

Page 266, add to note 63:

State v Johnson, 133 Wis 2d 207, 395 NW2d 176 (1986) (defendant's introduction of correspondence with psychiatrist and psychologist at postconviction hearing waived privilege as to these persons on issue of competence to stand trial at retrial).

Page 267, add to note 66:

Granviel v State, 723 SW2d 141 (Tex Crim App 1986) (warnings not required where examination was requested by defendant and defense counsel was present during examination).

§11.10 —Testimony

Page 268, add to note 75:

State v Correll, 148 Ariz 468, 715 P2d 721 (1986) (extrajudicial communication by psychiatrist to judge that more extensive competence evaluation was not necessary did not violate right to confrontation); Hunter v State, 489 So 2d 1086 (1986) (testimony of psychiatrist, regarding competence to stand trial, that referred to concurring opinion by nontestifying psychiatrist was admissible); Sangster v State, 70 Md App 456, 521 A2d 811 (1987) (written psychiatric report on competence to stand trial did not violate hearsay rule or confrontation clause).

Page 268, add to note 82:

State v Hudson, 152 Ariz 121, 730 P2d 830 (1987) (no error found in trial court's limitation of expert testimony, on competence to stand trial before jury, that did not allow experts to testify regarding defendant's childhood or past hospitalizations).

12 Criminal Proceedings: Trial

§12.01 Insanity and Related Defenses

Page 274, add to note 1:

When psychiatric or psychological testimony is introduced to negate mens rea in the absence of an insanity defense or a recognized diminished capacity defense, courts have frequently been inclined to exclude this evidence as unhelpful or unfairly prejudicial. *See, e.g.,* United States v Hillsberg, 812 F2d 328 (7th Cir 1987); United States v Shorter, 809 F2d 54 (DC Cir 1987); United States v Vinieris, 611 F Supp 1046 (SDNY 1985); People v Low, 732 P2d 622 (Colo 1987); Seeglitz v State, 500 NE2d 144 (Ind 1986); State v Jackman, 396 NW2d 24 (Minn 1986); State v Waymire, 504 So 2d 953 (La Ct App 1987); State v Johnson, 317 NC 343, 346 SE2d 596 (1986); Pitts v State, 712 SW2d 563 (Tex Ct App 1986).

Page 274, add to note 7:

Sparr & Atkinson, *Posttraumatic Stress Disorder as an Insanity Defense: Medicolegal Quicksand,* 143 Am J Psychiatry 608 (1986) ("insanity defense is appropriate only in the rare instance that a dissociative episode related to posttraumatic stress disorder leads to unpremeditated criminal activity").

Page 275, add to note 8:

Breslau & Davis, *Posttraumatic Stress Disorder: The Etiologic Specificity of Wartime Stressors,* 144 Am J Psychiatry 578 (1987) (participation in atrocities and other specific combat experiences increased risk of posttraumatic stress disorder).

Page 275, add to note 11:

State v Hodges, 239 Kan 63, 716 P2d 563 (1986) (expert testimony on battered wife syndrome is helpful to dispel notion that battered woman is free to leave the relationship, and meets *Frye* test of general acceptance in relevant scientific community). *But see* Cleney v State, 256 Ga 123, 344 SE2d 216 (1986) (no error in excluding evidence of battered wife syndrome where purpose of testimony was to determine voluntariness of pretrial statements based on abuse by two prior spouses); State v Necaise, 466 So 2d 660 (La Ct App 1985) (psychiatric testimony on battered wife syndrome not admissible absent a plea of not guilty by reason of insanity); Fielder v State, 683 SW2d 565 (Tex Civ App 1985) (testimony on battered wife syndrome by expert who did not examine defendant, and was thus incapable of determining her mental state, was irrelevant to any issue before the jury, and not admissible on issue of self-defense). See generally Rosen, *The Excuse of Self-Defense: Correcting A Historical Accident on Behalf of Battered Women Who Kill,* 36 Am UL Rev 11 (1986); Note, *The Battered Women's Syndrome and Self-Defense: A Legal and Empirical Dissent,* 72 Va L Rev 619 (1986).

§12.02   Insanity Defense—The Legal Standard

Page 277, add to note 31:

For an overview of the changes in the insanity defense from state to state following *Hinckley, see* Callahan, Mayer & Steadman, *Insanity Defense Reform in the United States—Post-Hinckley,* 11 Mental Disability L Rep 54 (1987).

Page 278, add at end of section:

Since the preparation of the bound volume, New York (NY Penal Law §40.15 (McKinney Supp 1987)) and Texas (Tex Penal Code §8.01 (Vernon Supp 1987)) have adopted the *M'Naghten* test. Maryland (Md Health-Gen §12-108 (Supp 1986) has adopted the ALI test.

§12.03   —The Role of the Expert

Page 278, add to note 44:

United States v Brown, 792 F2d 466 (4th Cir 1986) (either lay or expert testimony may be used to raise an insanity defense); State v Bay, 150 Ariz 112, 722 P2d 280 (1986) (expert testimony is not necessary to raise an insanity defense); State v Evans, 203 Conn 212, 523 A2d 1306 (1987) (state need not introduce expert testimony to rebut defense experts on insanity defense); Commonwealth v Monico, 396 Mass 793, 488 NE2d 1168 (1986) (psychiatric testimony is not a requirement of raising an insanity defense); State v Zespy, 723 P2d 564 (Wyo 1986) (lay testimony may rebut psychiatric testimony that defendant was not mentally responsible for his or her conduct).

Page 279, add to note 51:

Resneck v State, 499 NE2d 230 (Ind 1986) (psychiatrist not disqualified from court appointment to examine defendant's sanity because psychiatrist was on the staff at an institution at which defendant had once been treated).

Page 280, add to note 52:

State v Gambrell, 318 NC 249, 347 SE2d 390 (1986) (sufficient preliminary showing made to require appointment of psychiatrist to assist defense, where defendant behaved bizarrely in court and experienced hallucinations on admission to hospital). See Note, *Expert Services and the Indigent Criminal Defendant: The Constitutional Mandate of Ake v Oklahoma*, 84 Mich L Rev 1326 (1986); Note, *The Right to a Partisan Psychiatric Expert: Might Indigency Preclude Insanity?*, 61 NYU L Rev 703 (1986).

Page 280, add to note 55:

Commonwealth v Monico, 396 Mass 793, 488 NE2d 1168 (1986) (qualification of psychologist as expert witness on question of criminal responsibility turns on actual experience rather than academic degrees).

§12.04 —Basis

Page 281, add to note 58:

Blake v Kemp, 758 F2d 523 (11th Cir 1985) (state's failure to provide psychiatrist with defendant's taped confession and written correspondence deprived defendant of meaningful psychiatric examination and thus effective assistance of counsel).

Page 281, add to note 59:

But see State v Hudson, 152 Ariz 121, 730 P2d 830 (1986) (no error in trial court's refusal to permit defense experts to describe the tests that formed the basis for their opinion).

§12.05   —Limitations

Page 282, add to note 62:

In addition to the Fifth Amendment's impact in the context of participation in a court-ordered examination, it also limits the inferences concerning sanity that may be drawn from silence following *Miranda* warnings. In Wainwright v Greenfield, 106 S Ct 634 (1986), the Supreme Court found constitutionally impermissible the prosecution's closing argument that the defendant's exercise of his right to remain silent indicated his sanity at the time of the offense.

Page 282, add to note 64:

Sturgis v Goldsmith, 796 F2d 1103 (9th Cir 1986); Hicks v State, 256 Ga 715, 352 SE2d 762 (1987); Commonwealth v Harvet, 397 Mass 803, 494 NE2d 382 (1986).

Page 282, add to note 65:

Porter v State, 492 So 2d 970 (Miss 1986).

Page 282, add to note 66:

Muhammad v State, 494 So 2d 969 (Fla 1986) (defendant who refused to speak with court-appointed psychiatrists not permitted to present expert testimony in support of insanity defense). *But see* Moss v State, 256 Ga 831, 353 SE2d 348 (1987) (defendant who invoked Fifth Amendment to refuse to participate in court-ordered psychiatric examination is entitled to present an insanity defense without the use of expert testimony).

Page 284, add to note 78:

United States v Wright, 783 F2d 1091 (DC Cir 1986) (no error in permitting government to ask codefendant's psychiatrist, on cross-examination, about basis for his opinion which included one defendant's statement to him that implicated codefendant); State v Duell, 332 SE2d 246 (W Va 1986) (defendant's psychiatrist should have been permitted to rely on tape-recorded examination of the defendant by the state's psychiatrist).

Page 284, add to note 80:

But see People v Furman, 158 Mich App 302, 404 NW2d 246 (1987) (no error in refusing to admit videotaped interview of defendant by defendant's psychiatrist).

§12.06 —Testimony

Page 285, add to note 86:

North Carolina v Spangler, 333 SE2d 722 (NC 1985) (it was appropriate to permit state's psychiatrist to testify that defendant did not lack the capacity to distinguish right from wrong with respect to killing someone rather than with reference to this particular victim); Russell v Texas, 694 SW2d 207 (Tex Civ App 1985) (defendant's conviction reversed where trial court improperly commented to jury that it was not bound by defense psychologist's opinion that defendant could not conform his behavior to the requirements of the law and was therefore insane).

Page 286, add to note 87:

United States v Hillsberg, 812 F2d 328 (7th Cir 1987) (Rule 704(b) prohibits a psychiatric opinion as to whether intoxication prohibited defendant from conforming his or her conduct to the requirements of the law); United States v Freeman, 804 F2d 1574 (11th Cir 1986) (704(b) does not unconstitutionally limit the right to present a defense); United States v Windfelder, 790 F2d 576 (7th Cir 1986) (704(b) limitations not applicable to the mental state of someone other than the defendant or testimony of a witness not qualified on the workings of the human mind); United States v Prickett, 790 F2d 35 (6th Cir 1986) (704(b) does not violate ex post facto clause); United States v Mest, 789 F2d 1069 (4th Cir 1986) (same); United States v Frisbee, 623 F Supp 1217 (D Cal 1985) (limitation of 704(b) permits experts to present only "diagnosis, the facts upon which their diagnoses are based, and the characteristics of any mental diseases or defects the experts believe the defendant possessed during the relevant time period").

Page 286, add to note 88:

People v Whitler, 171 Cal App 3d 337, 214 Cal Rptr 610 (1985) (§29 is constitutional); People v Sanders, 154 Cal App 3d 197, 201 Cal Rptr 411 (1984) (defense psychiatrist could state the effects of PCP generally and as to this witness, but not that as a result of PCP the defendant did not satisfy statutory intent or malice requirements); People v Jackson, 152 Cal App 3d 961, 199 Cal Rptr 848 (1984) (§29 does not deprive defendant of right to present a defense).

§12.08 —Capital Offenses

Page 290, add to note 103:

The reported decisions have not been rigorous in their scrutiny of the purported experts. Nethery v Texas, 692 SW2d 686 (Tex Crim App 1985) (psychiatrist who had examined 10,000 persons charged with criminal offenses, 850 charged with murder, 120 charged with capital murder, who in every capital murder case in which he testified about future dangerousness had testified in the affirmative, and who said he was 100% accurate in predictions notwithstanding contrary statements by American Psychiatric Association, was qualified to give expert testimony on future dangerousness).

Page 290, add to note 104:

California v Brown, 107 S Ct 837 (1987) (court's instruction to jury during penalty phase of a capital murder trial that jurors "must not be swayed by mere sentiment, conjecture, sympathy, passion, prejudice, public opinion or public feeling" did not violate Eighth or Fourteenth Amendments to the United States Constitution); Thigpen v Jones, 788 F2d 1101 (5th Cir 1986), *cert denied,* 55 USLW 3569 (US 1987) (defense counsel's unjustified failure to present evidence of defendant's mental disability in capital sentencing constituted reversible error).

Page 290, add at end of section:

In addition to the use of psychiatric and psychological evidence on prediction and mitigation issues, the Supreme Court's conclusion that execution of a prisoner who is insane violates the Eighth Amendment's ban on cruel and unusual punishment opens another avenue for psychiatric and psychological input into the sentencing process for capital offenses. *Ford v Wainwright,* 106 S Ct 2595 (1986).

§12.09 —Noncapital Offenses

Page 290, text, add after first paragraph of section:

The attempt to reduce discretion in sentencing has been furthered by the adoption of guidelines by the United States Sentencing Commission (created by 28 USC §991 *et seq*).

§12.12 —Limitations

Page 294, add to note 119:

But see Mahaffey v Broglin, 630 F Supp 1280 (ND Ind 1986) (psychiatric evaluation of defendant performed by court-appointed psychiatrist following defendant's raising of insanity defense, which was later withdrawn, may be introduced at sentencing without regard to failure to provide Fifth Amendment warnings at time of examination); State v Mercier, 128 NH 57, 509 A2d 1246 (1986) (*Estelle v Smith* not applicable to psychiatric examination ordered following insanity acquittal introduced at "non-punitive commitment" proceeding).

§12.13 —Testimony

Page 295, add at end of section:

Merely because a psychiatrist or psychologist testifies that the statutory criteria for certain sentencing provisions utilizing psychiatric diagnostic criteria are met, and is not contradicted by other experts, does not necessarily mean that the court will be bound by that conclusion. *See, e.g., State v Huntley*, 302 Or 418, 730 P2d 1234 (1986) (trial court not bound by psychiatrist's conclusion that defendant did not suffer from a personality disorder indicating a propensity for criminal activity within the contemplation of dangerous offender sentencing provision).

13 Legal Issues Involving Children

§13.01 Child Custody and Visitation—The Legal Standard

Page 302, add to note 8:

In re Adoption of JJ, 515 A2d 883 (Pa 1986) (termination of parental rights based on a mental or physical disability should focus on effect of the disability on parenting capacity and not mere existence of the disability).

Page 303, add to note 12:

See, e.g., In re Petition of DIS for the Adoption of SAD, 494 A2d 1316 (DC 1985); Warren v State, 501 So 2d 706 (Fla Dist Ct App 1987); MHB v HTB, 100 NJ 567, 498 A2d 775 (1985); Patzer v Glaser, 396 NW2d 740 (ND 1986).

§13.02 —The Role of the Expert

Page 303, add to note 16:

In re Teshea D, 9 Conn App 490, 519 A2d 1232 (1987) (testimony by mental health experts is not a requirement for decision addressing the best interests of the child in a termination proceeding).

Page 304, add to note 19:

Conservatorship of Ortiz, 190 Cal App 3d 50, 235 Cal Rptr 133 (1987) (testimony of psychiatrist concerning condition of severely disabled child was admissible in proceeding seeking conservatorship of child). See Ash & Guyer, *The Functions of Psychiatric Evaluation in Contested Child Custody and Visitation Cases*, 25 J Am Acad Child Psychiatry 554 (1986).

Page 304, add to note 23:

Aldrich v Aldrich, 505 So 2d 116 (La Ct App 1987) (psychologist is mental health professional within contemplation of rule providing for court-ordered mental evaluations in custody proceedings).

Page 304, add to note 24:

Golzband, *Should Adult Psychiatrists be Doing Child Custody Evaluations?*, 14 Bull Am Acad Psychiatry & L 361 (1986).

Page 305, add to note 25:

In re RA & VA, 225 Neb 157, 403 NW2d 357 (1987) (no abuse of discretion in ordering father to submit to psychological evaluation to determine custody or visitation issues). *But see In re* Evans, 81 NC App 449, 344 SE2d 325 (1986) (mother's refusal to participate in court-ordered psychiatric examination could not be basis for denial of custody).

Page 305, add to note 26:

Merl v Merl, 513 NYS2d 184 (1987) (no error in trial court's giving greater weight to treating psychiatrist's testimony than that of court-appointed psychiatrist); *In re* Elizabeth "Q", 511 NYS2d 181 (1987) (even though court-appointed psychiatrist initially thought he had been retained by county social services department, use of standard psychological tests and procedures did not establish bias justifying exclusion of testimony).

Page 305, add to note 30:

Kleber, Howell, & Tibbits-Kleber, *The Impact of Parental Homosexuality in Child Custody Cases: A Review of the Literature*, 14 Bull Am Acad Psychiatry & L 81 (1986).

§13.03 —Basis

Page 306, add to note 32:

Crum v Crum, 122 AD2d 771, 505 NYS2d 656 (1986) (it was not error to permit psychiatrist who had interviewed and observed father but not mother to offer opinion, particularly where mother had refused to meet with the psychiatrist).

§13.04 —Limitations

Page 308, add to note 44:

Petitions of Dept of Social Servs, 399 Mass 279, 503 NE2d 1275 (1987) (psychotherapist-patient privilege does not require exclusion of entire hospital records because some psychiatric information is contained in such records); Clark v Clark, 220 Neb 771, 371 NW2d 749 (1985) (filing petition for dissolution of marriage in which fitness to have custody of child was alleged waived physician-patient privilege).

§13.09 —Limitations

Page 312, add to note 56:

The other side of this issue is presented by the situation of the defendant who seeks to discover records of treatment of the abused minor that might shed light on the existence of abuse or the credibility of the complaining minor. For example, in State v Pierson, 201 Conn 211, 514 A2d 724 (1986), the Supreme Court of Connecticut held that the state's presentation of the testimony of a therapist who had treated a child before and after an alleged sexual assault, to show the absence of any inconsistencies in the child's complaint, did not impliedly waive the privilege as to treatment of the child generally. The court did rule, however, under the confrontation clause, that a more limited inquiry was required into the possibility that the therapist possessed information about the mental condition of the complainant that might be admissible for impeachment of the complainant. *See also* Kansas v Munyon, 726 P2d 1333 (Kan 1986) (institution of criminal prosecution for sexual assault of child did not waive psychologist-patient privilege as to communications between psychologist, child, and child's mother, who was defendant's former wife).

Page 312, add to note 57:

In Pennsylvania v Ritchie, 107 S Ct 989 (1987), the Supreme Court concluded that those portions of state files containing investigations of child abuse that reveal information favorable to the accused and that might reasonably affect the outcome of the case if admitted into evidence must be turned over to the defendant. Professional liability for reporting suspected instances of child abuse appears to be limited by the conferral of absolute immunity for these reports. Storch v Silverman, 213 Cal Rptr 27 (Ct App 1986).

§13.10 —Testimony

Page 313, add to note 65:

See Milner, Gold, & Wimberly, *Prediction and Explanation of Child Abuse: Cross-Validation of the Child Abuse Potential Inventory*, 54 J Cons Clinical Psychology 865 (1986).

Page 315, add to note 70:

But see State v Friedrich, 135 Wis 2d 1, 398 NW2d 763 (1987) (no abuse of discretion by trial court in excluding expert testimony that defendant did not conform to psychological profile of incestuous sex abusers, in light of risk that testimony would usurp function of the jury).

Page 315, add to note 71:

Particularly in the case of sexual assaults against minors, courts are more willing to admit evidence of other similar acts without regard to the risks that such evidence may be used for conformity purposes. State v DeLeonardo, 340 SE2d 350 (NC 1986) (in prosecution of defendant for performing anal intercourse on 9- and 12-year old sons, prosecution permitted to introduce evidence of attempted vaginal intercourse with 3-year-old daughter); State v Fishnick, 127 Wis 2d 247, 378 NW2d 272 (1985) (in prosecution of defendant for fondling 3-year-old girl, prosecution permitted to introduce evidence of defendant's request to 13-year-old girl one week earlier to expose herself).

Page 316, add to note 77:

United States v Short, 790 F2d 464 (6th Cir 1986) (testimony of social worker describing three-year-old child's play with anatomically correct dolls not hearsay when introduced to prove child's mental state regarding knowledge of oral sex); *In re* ME & LE v MEE, 715 SW2d 572 (Mo Ct App 1986) (testimony of family service worker about child's statements and actions in play with anatomically correct dolls not hearsay, as not introduced for truth of matter asserted, but to prove sexual knowledge inappropriate to age); *In re* Penelope B, 104 Wash 2d 643, 709 P2d 1185 (1985) (child's conduct during play therapy was nonassertive conduct and thus not hearsay). See White, *Interviewing Young Sexual Abuse Victims with Anatomically Correct Dolls,* 10 Child Abuse & Neglect 519 (1986) (in a comparison of structured interviews of children with anatomically correct dolls, children who had been referred for investigation of sexual abuse displayed significantly more sexually related behaviors than children who had not been referred for investigation of sexual abuse). See also Hibbard, Roghmann, & Hoeklman, *Genitalia in Children's Drawings: An Association With Sexual Abuse,* 79 J Am Acad Pediatrics 129 (1987) (study of children aged 3 to 7 known to have been abused showed 6.8 times greater likelihood of drawing genitalia on human figures than control group).

Page 316, add to note 78:

Oldsen v People, 732 P2d 1132 (Colo 1986) (child's statement to physician concerning abuse did not meet Rule 803(4) requirements where it was not shown that she understood the need to provide accurate information for medical treatment).

Page 316, add to note 79:

MED v JPM, 3 Va App 391, 350 SE2d 215 (1986) (statement by child to psychologist describing sexual abuse by father was type of information normally used by experts as basis for opinion).

Page 316, add to note 81:

United States v Dorian, 803 F2d 1439 (8th Cir 1986) (five-year-old child's out-of-court statement to stepmother about sexual abuse by father fell within catchall exception to hearsay rule); Oldsen v People, 732 P2d 1132 (Colo 1986) (child's statements to physician, psychologist, and social worker identifying father as assailant qualified for inclusion under residual exception to hearsay rule); *In re* Marriage of PKA & JEA, 725 SW2d 78 (Mo Ct App 1987) (child's statements to mother and psychologist about sexual abuse by father fell within special exception to hearsay rule); DAH v GAH, 371 NW2d 1 (Minn Ct App 1985) (child's out-of-court statements to psychologist during play therapy fell within catchall exception to hearsay rule); *In re* Penelope B, 104 Wash 2d 643, 709 P2d 1185 (1985) (child sex abuse hearsay exception only applies in criminal proceedings). See Comment, *Legislative Responses to Child Sex Abuse Cases: The Hearsay Exception and the Videotape Deposition,* 34 Cath UL Rev 1021 (1985).

Page 317, add to note 82:

United States v Azure, 801 F2d 336 (6th Cir 1986) (expert on child abuse not permitted to give opinion that child's story was credible); State v Lindsey, 149 Ariz 472, 720 P2d 72 (1986) (expert testimony that very small percentage of incest victims lie usurps function of jury); Russell v State, 289 Ark 533, 712 SW2d 916 (1986) (expert should not be permitted to testify that child's statements were consistent with abuse); People v Higa, 735 P2d 203 (Colo Ct App 1987) (error to permit psychiatrist to opine that child was being truthful in allegations of sexual assault); Butler v State, 178 Ga App 110, 342 SE2d 338 (1986) (admission of pediatrician's testimony that, although there was no medical evidence of trauma to genitalia, child was abused because children do not lie about such matters, with which they have no experience, was reversible error); State v Myers, 382 NW2d 91 (Iowa

1986) (expert witness testimony that children typically are truthful in reports of sexual abuse should be excluded because it is not helpful to jury and improperly suggests that complainant is telling the truth and thus defendant is guilty); State v Jackson, 239 Kan 463, 721 P2d 232 (1986) (expert on child abuse not permitted to testify that children were telling truth and that defendant committed acts charged); State v Kim, 318 NC 614, 350 SE2d 347 (1986) (child psychologist's testimony that child who claimed to be victim of sexual assault had not lied to psychologist was inadmissible character evidence to support child's credibility); Commonwealth v Seese, 512 Pa 439, 517 A2d 920 (1986) (expert testimony that eight-year-olds do not lie about sexual abuse was impermissible encroachment on province of jury); Garcia v State, 712 SW2d 249 (Tex App 1986) (expert on child sexual assault not permitted to testify that children do not lie about being sexually abused).

Page 317, add to note 83:

United States v St Pierre, 812 F2d 417 (8th Cir 1987) (expert permitted to testify to common characteristics of sexually abused children); State v Moran, 151 Ariz 378, 728 P2d 248 (1986) (expert testimony explaining why recantation is not inconsistent with occurrence of abuse is admissible as helpful to jury, but testimony that child is truthful and was abused is not admissible); Poyner v State, 705 SW2d 882 (Ark 1986) (expert testimony about typical behavior of abused children relevant to explain childrens' failure to come forward with complaint until after parents separated); People v Gray, 187 Cal App 3d 213, 231 Cal Rptr 658 (1987) (expert testimony on child sexual abuse accommodation syndrome admissible to explain delayed reporting and inconsistency of complaint); Kruse v State, 483 So 2d 1383 (Fla Dist Ct App 1986) (expert testimony that child victim of sexual assault suffered from posttraumatic stress disorder did not invade province of jury); Allison v State, 346 SE2d 380 (Ga Ct App 1986) (expert permitted to testify to child sexual abuse accommodation syndrome, behaviors typical of children who have been sexually abused, as helpful to jury in evaluating victim's credibility); State v Clements, 241 Kan 77, 734 P2d 1096 (1987) (treating therapist permitted to testify that child's progress in therapy was consistent with child's claim of sodomy); State v Meyers, 359 NW2d 604 (Minn 1984) (expert permitted to describe typical behavior of sexually abused children because jury is not likely to be familiar with specific aspects of victim's behavior); State v Geyman, 729 P2d 475 (Mont 1986) (expert permitted to testify that children generally do not make up stories of sexual abuse, and that child in instant case was credible and was sexually abused); People v Keindl, 502 NE2d 577, 509 NYS2d 790 (1986) (no abuse of discretion found in trial court's permitting expert to testify to typical reactions of children who are sexually abused by stepparents, as this is not something within knowledge of average juror). *But see* cases cited *supra* note 82. *See also* Lantrip v Commonwealth, 713 SW2d 816 (1986) (testimony of expert on child sexual abuse accommodation syndrome not admissible in absence of proof of scientific acceptance by clinical psychologists and psychiatrists).

For an excellent analysis of the cases and the scientific research bearing on this issue, see McCord, *Expert Testimony About Child Complaints in Sexual Abuse Prosecutions: A Foray into the Admissibility of Novel Psychological Evidence*, 77 J Crim L & Criminology 1 (1986). *See also* Note, *The Unreliability of Expert Testimony on the Typical Characteristics of Sexual Abuse Victims*, 74 Geo LJ 429 (1985).

Page 317, add to note 84:

But see State v RW, 104 NJ 14, 514 A2d 1287 (1986) (no abuse of discretion in failing to order psychiatric examination of three-year-old alleged victim of sexual assault, in absence of a "substantial need" for psychiatric assistance in assessing credibility of a witness; such need may not be found based on extreme youth alone); State v Logue, 372 NW2d 151, 155-56 (ND 1985) (no abuse of discretion in denying psychiatric examination of four-year-old alleged victim of sexual assault, in absence of claim or showing of "mental or moral delusions or tendencies which would distort the imagination and would affect the probable credibility of the complaining witness"); State v Hiatt, 33 Or 60, 733 P2d 1373 (1987) (provisions of evidence code authorizing admission of expert testimony and excluding incompetent witnesses do not imply the right to order a pretrial examination of alleged victim in a sex abuse case).

14

Personal Injury Litigation

§14.02   Mental and Emotional Consequences of Physical Injuries—The Legal Standard

Page 323, add to note 1:

Modaber v Kelley, 232 Va 60, 348 SE2d 233 (1986) (injury to an unborn child constitutes injury to mother such that mother may recover for physical injury and mental suffering associated with a stillbirth).

§14.03   —The Role of the Expert

Page 324, add to note 5:

Stafford v Neurological Medicine, Inc, 811 F2d 470 (8th Cir 1987) (testimony of geriatric psychiatrist that diagnosis of brain tumor made for insurance purpose, when learned of by deceased, caused an impulse disorder that was cause of suicide, met standard for submission of case to jury). *See* Curry v Giant Food Co, 522 A2d 1283 (DC Ct App 1987) (exclusion of testimony of physician who had one year of psychiatric training 40 years ago, when offered on issue of foreseeability of acquiring an alcoholic habit following an arrest and forcible detention, was proper).

Page 325, add to note 17:

Howle v PYA/Monarch, Inc, 288 SC 586, 344 SE2d 157, 161 (Ct App 1986) ("psychologist, once qualified as an expert witness by reason of education, training, and experience, is competent to testify as to diagnosis, prognosis, and causation of mental and emotional disturbance").

Page 325, add to note 18:

GIW S Valve C v Smith, 471 So 2d 81 (Fla Dist Ct App 1985) (reversible error to admit, over objection, testimony of a witness who was a clinical psychologist and clinical neuropsychologist on issue of prognosis for future physiological effects of accident upon plaintiff's brain). *But see* Westinghouse Elec Corp v Lawrence, 488 So 2d 623 (Fla Dist Ct App 1986) (clinical psychologist was competent to state opinion regarding causal relationship between claimant's mental disorder or condition and physical injuries sustained in industrial accident).

Page 325, add to note 19:

Johnson v Verrilli, 134 Misc 2d 582, 511 NYS2d 1008 (1987) (plaintiff entitled to recover for serious personal injuries in stillbirth of her child as a result of defendant's malpractice, including posttraumatic stress disorder and mental anguish). See Kuch, Swinson, & Kirby, *Post-Traumatic Stress Disorder After Car Accidents*, 30 Can J Psychiatry 426 (1985).

§14.04   Emotional Assaults—The Legal Standard

Page 326, add to note 25:

Asuncion v Columbia Hosp for Women, 514 A2d 1187 (DC 1986) (mother who brought medical malpractice action alleging she suffered emotional distress did not state a claim for negligent infliction of emotional distress, in that no physical injury occurred).

Page 326, add to note 27:

Whalley v Sakura, 804 F2d 580 (10th Cir 1986) (only some physical manifestation or injury resulting from the emotional injury is required); Champion v Gray, 478 So 2d 17 (Fla 1985) (impact rule modified to recognize a claim for damages flowing from a significant, discernible physical injury, when that injury is the foreseeable result of defendant's negligence); Quill v Trans World Airlines, 361 NW2d 438 (Minn Ct App 1985) (airline passenger, who suffered severe mental distress when plane dove 34,000 feet in an uncontrolled tailspin, permitted to recover for mental distress in the absence of severe physical manifestation of mental injuries suffered); State v Eaton, 101 Nev 705, 710 P2d 1370 (1985) (recognition of a cause of action for serious emotional distress manifested by physical symptoms caused by apprehending the death or serious injury of a loved one due to the defendant's negligence).

Page 327, add to note 30:

Grandstaff v City of Borger, 767 F2d 161 (5th Cir 1985) (victim's widow and stepsons, as bystanders, entitled to recover damages under Texas law for negligent infliction of emotional distress); Hinojosa v South Texas Drilling & Exploration, Inc, 727 SW2d 320 (Tex Civ App 1987) (in suit to recover for negligent infliction of emotional distress, close friend of decedent, who heard friend fall and saw his body, was not entitled to recover for negligent infliction of emotional distress as a bystander, because he had no familial relationship with decedent); Gates v Richardson, 719 P2d 193 (Wyo 1986) (plaintiff who witnessed a serious accident or its aftermath, involving bodily harm or death, may recover).

Page 327, add to note 31:

Kossel v Superior Court, 186 Cal App 3d 1060, 231 Cal Rptr 183 (1986) (the court narrowly defined what is required to be a "direct victim" under *Molien;* a reasonable foreseeability that plaintiff will hear about a misdiagnosis of a spouse's illness and a reasonable probability that the misdiagnosis will cause her great mental distress, is not enough).

§14.05 —The Role of the Expert

Page 328, add to note 35:

Beaber, Marston, Michelli, & Mills, *A Brief Test for Measuring Malingering in Schizophrenic Individuals,* 142 Am J Psychiatry 1478 (1985); Kowitt, *Rorschach Content in Post-Traumatic Stress Disorders: A Reply to Carr,* 49 J Personality Assessment 21 (1985).

Page 328, add to note 36:

But see Mart v Hill, 505 So 2d 1120, 1126 (La 1987) (psychiatrist, who testified he was "trained to ferret out and recognize malingerers," and that plaintiff's pain syndrome was real, used to support disability determination).

§14.10 Workers' Compensation—The Legal Standard

Page 333, add to note 53:

Zabkowicz v West Bend Co, 789 F2d 540 (7th Cir 1986) (emotional trauma as result of sexual harassment is compensable under Wisconsin Workers Compensation Act); Malik v Apex Intl Alloys, Inc, 762 F2d 77 (10th Cir 1985) (damages for mental anguish recoverable without proving accompanying physical injury under Workers Compensation Act, when employee intentionally discharged for filing worker's compensation claim); Battista v Chrysler Corp, 517 A2d 295 (Del Super Ct 1986) (psychological injuries caused by wrongful demotion and verbal abuse compensable in absence of a physical injury); Jackco Painting Contractors v Industrial Commn, 710 P2d 755 (Colo Ct App 1985) (decedent worker's dependents entitled to compensation where work-related injury caused a mental condition which proximately caused worker's suicide); Peters v Michigan Bell Tel Co, 423 Mich 594, 377 NW2d 774, 776 (1985) (proof of causal nexus for compensability of mental disorder under workers compensation requires finding that "1) the claimant was disabled; 2) an injury in the form of a precipitating work-related event had occurred; 3) using a subjective causal nexus standard, the employment had combined with some internal weakness or disease to produce the disability").

Page 333, add to note 56:

Martin v Rhode Island Pub Transit Auth, 506 A2d 1365 (RI 1986) (malicious three-month harassment campaign by fellow employees met requirements for stress beyond that normally encountered in workplace in case in which no physical injury is present). *But see* City of Aurora v Industrial Commn, 710 P2d 1122 (Colo Ct App 1985) (mental disability arising as an occupational disease from conditions of employment, rather than as a result of an accident or physical trauma, is compensable); Ryan v Connor, 28 Ohio St 3d 406, 503 NE2d 1379 (1986) (heart attack and resulting death compensable where related to forced early retirement). *See* Comment, *Workers' Compensation and Gradual Stress in the Workplace*, 133 U Pa L Rev 847 (1985); Comment, *Workers Compensation: Compensating Claimants Who Suffer Psychological Disabilities Caused Solely by Job Related Mental Stress*, 60 Tul L Rev 651 (1986).

Page 333, add to note 58:

Magouirk v United Parcel Serv, 495 So 2d 55 (Ala Civ App 1986) (mental disability caused by stress of employment without a physical injury is not compensable); Johnson v State, 219 Neb 457, 364 NW2d 1 (1985) (no recovery permitted for mental injuries in absence of a proven physical injury).

Page 334, add to note 62:

Williams v State, 489 So 2d 461 (La Ct App 1986) (claimant who has a mental condition that results in a belief that he is disabled entitled to compensation).

Page 334, add to note 63:

Spencer v Industrial Commn, 733 P2d 158 (Utah 1987).

§14.11 —The Role of the Expert

Page 334, add to note 64:

Harvey v Raleigh Police Dept, 355 SE2d 147 (NC Ct App 1987) (psychological autopsy admissible in worker's compensation proceeding).

Page 334, add to note 67:

GIW S Valve Co v Smith, 471 So 2d 81 (Fla Dist Ct App 1985) (reversible error to admit, over objection, testimony of a witness who was a clinical psychologist and clinical neuropsychologist on issue of prognosis for future physiological effects of accident upon plaintiff's brain); Fierro v Stanley's Hardware, 104 NM 401, 722 P2d 652 (1985) (psychologist may not testify as to causal connection between an accident and psychological disability, under provisions of New Mexico Workmen's Compensation Act). *But see* Westinghouse Elec Corp v Lawrence, 488 So 2d 623 (Fla Dist Ct App 1986) (clinical psychologist was competent to state opinion regarding causal relationship between claimant's mental disorder or condition and physical injuries sustained in industrial accident).

§14.12 —Basis

Page 335, add to note 68:

But see Harvey v Raleigh Police Dept, 355 SE2d 147 (NC Ct App 1987) (error to disregard psychological autopsy in determination of deceased's state of mind and effect of work-related stress at time of death, in workers compensation claim by widow).

§14.13 —Limitations

Page 335, add to note 71:

But see Bobo v State, 256 Ga 357, 349 SE2d 690 (1986) (police officer did not waive psychiatrist-patient privilege by allowing testimony concerning her psychiatric examination following shooting incident to be made public in her workers compensation case).

§14.14   —Testimony

Page 336, add to note 76:

But see Paco v American Leather Mfg Co, 213 NJ Super 90, 516 A2d 623 (1986) (no contravention of the spirit and purpose of the workers compensation act to require petitioner, in a formal hearing, to bring in a medical witness, as opposed to submitting medical reports).

Page 336, add to note 78:

Howard v Superior Contractors, 180 Ga App 68, 348 SE2d 563 (1986); Bigler v Workers' Compensation Bd, 96 Pa Commw 642, 508 A2d 635 (1986).

Page 336, add to note 81:

But see Bruckner v Workman's Compensation Appeal Bd, 521 A2d 980 (Pa Commw Ct 1987) (referee's decision dismissing claim supported by psychiatrist's testimony that was equivocal, and accepting testimony of employer's psychiatrist that to a reasonable degree of medical certainty manic-depressive illness was not related to events in teacher's classroom, was not error).

§14.15   Social Security Disability Benefits—The Legal Standard

Page 337, add to note 94:

The provisions of the Social Security Disability Benefits Reform Act of 1984 include the requirement of promulgation of new mental impairment criteria. Final regulations have been published at 50 Fed Reg 35,038 (1985) and will be codified at 20 CFR 404, subt P, app 1. The regulations are designed to bring the disability criteria in closer harmony with DSM-III. *See* Bowen v City of NY, 106 S Ct 2022 (1986).

Page 338, add to note 95:

Poulin v Bowen, 817 F2d 865 (DC Cir 1987) (appellant's ability to work for brief periods between symptoms of chronic schizophrenia did not prevent him from meeting severity requirement of revised listing in § 12.03).

Page 339, add to note 96:

Benson v Heckler, 780 F2d 16 (8th Cir 1985) (nonpsychotic mental disorders may be disabling).

Page 339, add to note 99:

However, in Bowen v Yuckert, 55 USLW 4735 (US 1987), the Supreme Court determined that the HHS severity regulations permitting a denial of a disability claim based on medical evidence alone, without regard to age, education, or work experience, were facially valid and did not conflict with the definition of *disability* set forth in the Social Security Act.

§14.16 —The Role of the Expert

Page 340, add to note 109:

Sprague v Bowen, 812 F2d 1226 (9th Cir 1987) (widow's treating physician for past 25 years was qualified to give opinion on widow's mental state and its impact on her physical disability, even though he was not a psychiatrist); Ceballos v Bowen, 649 F Supp 693 (SDNY 1986) (treating physician's report may not be discounted by administrative law judge without first providing disability claimant notice of proposed action and an opportunity to submit a more detailed statement).

§14.19 —Testimony

Page 342, add to note 126:

Evosevich v Consolidation Coal Co, 789 F2d 1021 (3d Cir 1986) (written report of nonexamining physician admissible in an administrative hearing on black lung benefits claim); Sprague v Bowen, 812 F2d 1226 (9th Cir 1987) (widow's treating physician qualified to give opinion on impact of her mental state on her physical disability, even though he was not a psychiatrist).

15 Competence

§15.04 —Limitations

Page 354, add to note 18:

In re Estate of Moorman, 709 SW2d 160 (Mo Ct App 1986) (psychiatrist permitted to testify about patient's competence under an exception to physician-patient privilege following prima facie showing of incapacity through other evidence). *But see In re* KS, 405 NW2d 78 (Wis 1987) (exception to physician-patient and psychologist-patient privilege applicable in involuntary hospitalization proceedings does not apply in guardianship or protective placement proceedings).

Page 354, add to note 19:

Conservatorship of Torres, 180 Cal App 3d 1159, 1163, 226 Cal Rptr 142 (1986) (psychiatrist's testimony admissible over objection that psychiatrist's use of hearsay permitted otherwise inadmissible evidence to be received and that expert testimony unnecessary on issue of ability of conservatee to care for himself). *But see* Hirdler v Boyd, 702 SW2d 727 (Tex Civ App 1985, writ refd nre) (letter from physician, written in response to a request from patient's attorney, regarding mental health of patient was not a medical or business record admissible under hearsay exception).

Page 355, add to note 24:

Mo Ann Stat §475.075(1) (Vernon 1987) (1983 amendment rewrote section, and 1985 amendment changed and embellished some wording, but basic import of statute has not changed substantively).

§15.06   Testamentary Capacity—The Legal Standard

Page 356, add to note 34:

But see Barnes v Willis, 497 So 2d 90 (Ala 1986) (execution of will by testator while ward of county probate court has no legal effect).

§15.07   —The Role of the Expert

Page 358, add to note 42:

In re Swain, 125 AD2d 574, 509 NYS2d 643 (1986) (testimony of psychiatrist that testatrix did not know nature of her assets or objects of her bounty, based solely on an examination of medical records, was speculative and did not rebut testimony of treating physician, who found testatrix rational and lucid at all times he saw her).

§15.11   Contractual Capacity—The Legal Standard

Page 361, add to note 68:

McGovern v State Employees Retirement Bd, 512 Pa 377, 517 A2d 523 (1986) (prior to death, best determination of requisite mental capacity to execute retirement application is based on testimony of persons who observed decedent's conduct on date in question, rather than testimony as to observations made prior to and subsequent to that date).

§15.13   —Basis

Page 363, add to note 79:

McAllister v Schettler, 521 A2d 617 (Del Ch 1986) (though vendor of land had been known to be mentally impaired in the past, evidence of competence on date contract was executed was equally persuasive).

16 Civil Commitment

§16.01 The Legal Standard

Page 369, add to note 1:

See generally Morris, *The Supreme Court Examines Civil Commitment Issues: A Retrospective and Prospective Assessment,* 60 Tul L Rev 927 (1986).

Page 369, add to note 2:

People v Lang, 113 Ill 2d 407, 498 NE2d 1105 (1986) (mental illness for purposes of civil commitment proceeding is not tied to DSM-III classifications and includes person found unfit to stand trial).

Page 370, add to note 6:

In re LaBelle, 107 Wash 2d 196, 728 P2d 138 (1986) (grave disability portion of Washington commitment statute held constitutional). See also Bloom & Faulkner, *Competency Determinations in Civil Commitment,* 144 Am J Psychiatry 193 (1987).

§16.02 —The Role of the Expert

Page 371, add to note 14:

But see State v Putonki, 200 Conn 208, 510 A2d 1329 (1986) (in commitment proceedings following insanity acquittal, court is not bound by testimony of two psychiatrists who recommended release).

Page 372, add to note 20:

But see McNiel & Binder, *Predictive Validity of Judgments of Dangerousness in Emergency Civil Commitment,* 144 Am J Psychiatry 197 (1987) (study of emergency commitments, suggesting that this context permits valid predictions of short-term dangerousness).

Page 372, add to note 21:

See *In re* LR, 146 Vt 17, 497 A2d 753 (1985) (applying Barefoot v Estelle, 463 US 880 (1984), in the context of civil commitment).

§16.03 —Basis

Page 373, add to note 26:

In re Brown, 126 NH 309, 493 A2d 447 (1985) (psychiatrist's 35- to 40-minute examination and review of medical records was not constitutionally insufficient to support a commitment order). *But see In re* LR, 146 Vt 17, 497 A2d 753 (1985) (psychiatrist may base prediction of future behavior on hypothetical question rather than personal examination).

§16.04 —Limitations

Page 374, add to note 30:

In re Kenneth M, 130 Misc 2d 217, 495 NYS2d 131 (1985) (privilege against self-incrimination applicable to civil commitment proceedings).

Page 374, add to note 31:

Although the United States Supreme Court has not ruled on this precise question, it recently held that the Fifth Amendment guarantee against compulsory self-incrimination is not applicable in a proceeding for involuntary hospitalization of sexually dangerous persons, because the purpose of the proceeding is to treat and not to punish. Allen v Illinois, 106 S Ct 2988 (1986). *See also In re* Appeal in Pima County Mental Health Case No MH 1717, 149 Ariz 594, 721 P2d 142 (1986) (privilege against self-incrimination not applicable to mental health examination in commitment proceeding); People v Saribeyoglu, 131 Misc 2d 647, 501 NYS2d 286 (1986) (patient in civil commitment proceeding could not refuse to be a witness, but could refuse to answer questions that would incriminate him for criminal activity); State v Mercier, 128 NH 57, 509 A2d 1246 (1986) (privilege against self-incrimination not applicable in psychiatric examination, following verdict of not guilty by reason of insanity, to determine whether defendant should be committed or released).

But see Miller, Maier, & Kaye, *Miranda Comes to the Hospital: The Right to Remain Silent in Civil Commitment,* 142 Am J Psychiatry 1074 (1985) (study of consequences of giving Fifth Amendment warnings to patients regarding use of their statements in commitment hearings revealed that warnings had little impact on patient's willingness to speak with staff).

Page 375, add to note 34:

In re Appeal in Pima County Mental Health Case No MH 1717, 149 Ariz 594, 721 P2d 142 (1986) (physician-patient privilege not applicable in court-ordered examination in civil commitment proceeding).

Page 375, add to note 35:

Department of Youth Servs v A Juvenile, 398 Mass 516, 499 NE2d 812 (1986) (failure to inform juvenile that conversation with psychiatrist would not be confidential and would be used against juvenile in commitment proceeding precludes use of testimony by that psychiatrist); *In re* Pritchett, 499 NE2d 1029 (Ill App Ct 1986) (failure to inform patient of right to refuse to participate in examination and possibility of disclosure of results of examination at trial harmless error where patient refused to speak with examiner, who relied on other information as basis for opinion).

Page 376, add to note 42:

In re Samuels, 507 A2d 150 (DC Ct App 1986) (psychiatrist was entitled to rely on medical records of patient's previous hospitalizations and diagnosis and jury was entitled to learn of information upon which resulting diagnosis was based); People v Lang, 113 Ill 2d 407, 498 NE2d 1105 (1986) (expert witness in civil commitment proceeding may rely upon prior psychological evaluations, staff reports, and other medical records not admitted in evidence and may reveal content of these materials to explain basis for resulting opinion).

17

Novel Applications of Psychiatric and Psychological Evidence

§17.01 Testimonial Credibility—The Legal Standard

Page 382, add to note 2:

Zabrani v Riveron, 495 So 2d 1195 (Fla Dist Ct App 1986) (witness who had been found not guilty by reason of insanity was not thereby rendered incompetent as a witness, but this finding was relevant and admissible on the question of credibility).

Page 383, add to note 6:

Allison v State, 256 Ga 851, 353 SE2d 805 (1987) (expert testimony on child sexual abuse syndrome that opined that child was definitely abused invades province of jury); State v Myers, 382 NW2d 91 (Iowa 1986) (expert witness testimony that children typically are truthful in reports of sexual abuse should be excluded because it is not helpful to jury and improperly suggests that complainant is telling the truth, and thus that defendant is guilty); State v Kim, 318 NC 614, 350 SE2d 347 (1986) (psychologist's testimony that child victim of sexual assault had not lied to psychologist was inadmissible character evidence to support victim's credibility); State v Percy, 507 A2d 955 (Vt 1986) (expert testimony that rapists typically claim consent or amnesia, implying that a defendant who made both these claims is not believable, is not relevant to specific defendant who claimed both and, if relevant, is outweighed by danger of unfair prejudice).

Page 383, add to note 7:

United States v Blade, 811 F2d 461 (8th Cir 1987); Johnson v Wainwright, 806 F2d 1479 (11th Cir 1986); United States v Langford, 802 F2d 1176 (9th Cir 1986); United States v Serna, 799 F2d 842 (2d

Cir 1986); United States v Moore, 786 F2d 1308 (5th Cir 1986); State v Kemp, 199 Conn 473, 507 A2d 1387 (1986); State v Wheaton, 240 Kan 345, 729 P2d 1183 (1986); State v Mims, 501 So 2d 962 (La Ct App 1987); Bloodsworth v State, 307 Md 164, 512 A2d 1056 (1986); State v Cooper, 708 SW2d 299 (Mo Ct App 1986); State v Fontaine, 382 NW2d 374 (ND 1986); State v Buell, 22 Ohio St 3d 124, 489 NE2d 795 (1986). See Comment, *Admission of Expert Testimony on Eyewitness Identification,* 73 Cal L Rev 1402 (1985).

Page 383, add to note 8:

State v Moon, 45 Wash App 692, 726 P2d 1263 (1986).

Page 383, add to note 9:

Eiler v State, 63 Md App 439, 492 A2d 1320 (1985) (psychosis and paranoid schizophrenia); Pennsylvania v Mason, 518 A2d 282 (Pa Super Ct 1986) (paranoid schizophrenia, depression, and mild mental retardation).

Page 383, add to note 10:

State v Halstead, 362 NW2d 504 (Iowa 1985) (borderline mental retardation and deficit disorder).

§17.02   —The Role of the Expert

Page 384, add to note 14:

Frazier & Borgida, *Rape Trauma Syndrome Evidence in Court,* 40 Am Psychology 984 (1985); Massaro, *Experts, Psychology, Credibility and Rape: The Rape Trauma Syndrome Issue and Its Implications for Expert Psychological Testimony,* 69 Minn L Rev 395 (1985); McCord, *The Admissibility of Expert Testimony Regarding Rape Trauma Syndrome in Rape Prosecutions,* 26 BCL Rev 1143 (1985); Note, *The Unreliability of Expert Testimony on the Typical Characteristics of Sexual Abuse Victims,* 74 Geo LJ 429 (1985).

Page 385, add to note 16:

Illinois v Server, 499 NE2d 1019 (Ill App Ct 1986); Simmons v State, 504 NE2d 575 (Ind 1987); State v McQuillen, 239 Kan 590, 721 P2d 740 (1986); State v Allewalt, 517 A2d 714 (Md 1986); People v Skinner, 153 Mich App 815, 396 NW2d 548 (1986); Commonwealth v Gallagher, 353 Pa Super 426, 510 A2d 735 (1986); Lessard v State, 719 P2d 227 (Wyo 1986).

Page 385, add to note 17:

State v Broadniak, 718 P2d 322 (Mont 1986) (expert testimony concerning rape trauma syndrome to bolster credibility of victim invaded province of the jury); State v Black, 46 Wash App 259, 730 P2d 698 (1986) (error to admit evidence of rape trauma syndrome in absence of evidence of acceptance in relevant scientific community).

Page 386, add to note 23:

Schooler, Gerhard, & Loftus, *Qualities of the Unreal,* 12 J Experimental Psychology 171 (1986).

§17.03 —Basis

Page 388, add to note 33:

State v Johnson, 714 So 2d 753, 758 (Mo Ct App 1986) (discretion exists to order examination of witness on competence issue but should not be exercised in case of "mere assertion of testimonial contradictions, emotional instability, mental aberration, or even insanity"). *But see* State v Hicks, 240 Kan 302, 729 P2d 1146 (1986) (court properly ordered psychiatric examination of victim/witness of assault who had been found incompetent to stand trial 20 years earlier; in light of finding by psychiatrist that witness was competent to testify to occurrence, trial court properly excluded introduction of 20-year-old report and finding of incompetence).

Page 388, add to note 34:

But see Sullivan v State, 818 F2d __ (8th Cir 1987) (no reversible error in trial court's failure to order examination by defense psychiatrist of child victim of sexual assault, where extensive opportunity to explore claim of fabrication was provided on cross-examination); State v RW, 104 NJ 14, 514 A2d 1287 (1986) (no abuse of discretion in failing to order psychiatric examination of three-year-old alleged victim of sexual assault, in absence of a "substantial need" for psychiatric assistance in assessing credibility of a witness; such need may not be found based on extreme youth alone); State v Hiatt, 33 Or 60, 733 P2d 1373 (1987) (provisions of evidence code authorizing admission of expert testimony and excluding incompetent witnesses do not imply the right to order a pretrial examination of alleged victim in a sex abuse case).

§17.04 —Limitations

Page 389, add to note 35:

United States v Friedman, 636 F Supp 462 (SDNY 1986) (psychotherapist-patient privilege protects against disclosure of contents of psychiatric records of prospective witness); People v Reber, 177 Cal App 3d

523, 223 Cal Rptr 139 (1986) (where records of alleged victims of sexual assault showed developmental handicap and chronic mental illness, good cause for discovery of records was shown); People v District Court, 719 P2d 722 (Colo 1986) (psychotherapist-patient privilege applicable to postassault psychotherapy records not waived by victim's testimony about assault, and argument that victim may have told therapist a different version of events does not justify disclosure or in camera inspection of these records); State v Pierson, 201 Conn 2d 211, 514 A2d 724 (1986) (trial court should conduct voir dire of complaining witness's therapist, who testified to elements relative to proof of the offense, to determine whether therapist had information relevant to impeachment of complaining witness); Bobo v State, 256 Ga 357, 349 SE2d 690 (1986) (although disclosure of witness's psychiatric records may in rare instances be compelled where necessity and inability to obtain substantially similar evidence is shown, "fishing expedition" does not justify compelled disclosure); People v Foggy, 149 Ill App 3d 599, 500 NE2d 1026 (1986) (absolute privilege resulting in trial court's refusal to conduct in camera hearing to determine whether rape victim made statements to counselor that would exculpate defendant was not unconstitutional); Eiler v State, 63 Md App 439, 492 A2d 1320 (1985) (although psychiatrist-patient privilege applied, court permitted disclosure of witness's psychiatric record to test credibility); Commonwealth v Giacalone, 24 Mass App 166, 507 NE2d 769 (1987) (preliminary showing necessary to permit in camera screening of victim's psychiatric records protected by privilege was not made where main issue at trial was accuracy of rape victim's identification of defendants and victim's trial testimony did not suggest lack of mental capacity); People v Knowell, 512 NYS2d 190 (App Div 1987) (error to fail to order production, for in camera inspection, of psychiatric records of sole eyewitness to murder who had history of psychiatric problems and hospitalizations).

§17.05   —Testimony

Page 389, add to note 36:

State v Buell, 22 Ohio St 3d 124, 489 NE2d 795 (1986) (expert could testify about variables that may affect eyewitness testimony generally, but may not testify that a particular witness not alleged to suffer from a physical or mental impairment is not credible).

§17.06 The Psychiatric Autopsy—The Legal Standard

Page 390, add to note 38:

Shafii, Carrigan, Whittinghill, & Derrick, *Psychological Autopsy of Completed Suicide in Children and Adolescents,* 142 Am J Psychiatry 1061 (1985).

Page 390, add to note 43:

Harvey v Raleigh Police Dept, 355 SE2d 147 (NC Ct App 1987) (error to disregard psychological autopsy in determination of deceased's state of mind and effect of work-related stress at time of death in workers compensation claim by widow). *But see* Thompson v Mayes, 707 SW2d 951 (Tex Civ App 1986) (trial court did not abuse its discretion in excluding evidence of psychological autopsy where issue was not whether decedent committed suicide, but whether decedent was involved in disappearance of his father two years before decedent's own suicide).

§17.08 —Basis

Page 392, add to note 47:

McGrady v United States, 650 F Supp 379 (DSC 1986) (opinion of psychiatrist who did not examine deceased, sought to be introduced on issue of deceased's dangerousness, based on review of historical facts in medical file, was too speculative to be received in evidence).

Page 392, add to note 48:

Ebert, *Guide to Conducting a Psychological Autopsy,* 18 Prof Psychology 52 (1987).

18

Nontestimonial Uses of Psychiatric and Psychological Evidence

§18.02   Jury Selection

Page 404, add to note 18:

M. Nietzal & R. Dillehay, Psychological Consultation in the Courtroom (1986).

Cases

Evosevich v Consolidation Coal Co, 789 F2d 1021 (3d Cir 1986) §14.19

Evans, *In re*, 81 NC App 449, 344 SE2d 325 (1986) §13.02

F

Fielder v State, 683 SW2d 565 (Tex Civ App 1985) §12.01

Fierro v Stanley's Hardware, 104 NM 401, 722 P2d 652 (1985) §14.11

Ford v Wainwright, 106 S Ct 2595 (1986) §12.08

G

Garcia v State, 712 SW2d 249 (Tex Crim App 1986) §13.10

Gates v Richardson, 719 P2d 193 (Wyo 1986) §14.04

GIW S Valve C v Smith, 471 So 2d 81 (Fla Dist Ct App 1985) §§14.03, 14.11

Grand Jury Subpoenas Duces Tecum Dated Jan 30, 1986, *In re*, 638 F Supp 794 (D Me 1986) §10.04

Grandstaff v City of Borger, 767 F2d 161 (5th Cir 1985) §14.04

Granviel v State, 723 SW2d 141 (Tex Crim App 1986) §11.09

H

Harvey v Raleigh Police Dept, 355 SE2d 147 (NC Ct App 1987) §§14.11, 14.12, 17.06

Heald v State, 492 NE2d 671 (Ind 1986) §9.07

Hicks v State, 256 Ga 715, 352 SE2d 762 (1987) §12.05

Hinojosa v South Texas Drilling & Exploration, Inc, 727 SW2d 320 (Tex Civ App 1987) §14.04

Hirdler v Boyd, 702 SW2d 727 (Tex Civ App 1985) §15.04

Howard v Superior Contractors, 180 Ga App 68, 348 SE2d 563 (1986) §14.14

Howle v PYA/Monarch, Inc, 288 SC 586, 344 SE2d 157 (Ct App 1986) §§8.02, 14.03

Hunter v State, 489 So 2d 1086 (1986) §11.10

I

Illinois v Server, 499 NE2d 1019 (Ill App Ct 1986) §17.02

Illinois Psychological Assn v Falk, 638 F Supp 876 (ND Ill 1986) §9.09

J

Jackco Painting Contractors v Industrial Commn, 710 P2d 755 (Colo Ct App 1985) §14.10

JJ, *In re* Adoption of, 515 A2d 883 (Pa 1986) §13.01

Johnson v State, 219 Neb 457, 364 NW2d 1 (1985) §14.10

Johnson v Verrilli, 134 Misc 2d 582, 511 NYS2d 1008 (1987) §14.03

Johnson v Wainwright, 806 F2d 1479 (11th Cir 1986) §17.01

People v Whitler, 171 Cal App
3d 337, 214 Cal Rptr 610
(1985) §§9.08, 12.06

Peters v Michigan Bell Tel Co,
423 Mich 594, 377 NW2d
774 (1985) §14.10

Pitts v State, 712 SW2d 563
(Tex Ct App 1986) §12.01

PKA & JEA, In re Marriage of,
725 SW2d 78 (Mo Ct App
1987) §13.10

Porter v State, 492 So 2d 970
(Miss 1986) §12.05

Poulin v Bowen, 817 F2d 865
(DC Cir 1987) §14.15

Poyner v State, 705 SW2d 882
(Ark 1986) §13.10

Pritchett, In re, 499 NE2d 1029
(Ill App Ct 1986) §16.04

Psychiatric Inst of Wash v Allen,
509 A2d 619 (DC Ct App
1986) §§7.04, 9.07

Q

Quill v Trans World Airlines,
361 NW2d 438 (Minn Ct App
1985) §14.04

Quinn v Kent Gen Hosp, 617 F
Supp 1226 (D Del 1985)
§10.01

R

RA & VA, In re, 225 Neb 157,
403 NW2d 357 (1987) §13.02

Resneck v State, 499 NE2d 230
(Ind 1986) §12.03

Robinson v Commonwealth, 399
Mass 131, 503 NE2d 31
(1987) §10.02

Russell v State, 289 Ark 533,
712 SW2d 916 (1986) §13.10

Russell v Texas, 694 SW2d 207
(Tex Civ App 1985) §12.06

Ryan v Connor, 28 Ohio St 3d
406, 503 NE2d 1379 (1986)
§14.10

S

Samuels, In re, 507 A2d 150
(DC Ct App 1986) §16.04

Sangster v State, 70 Md App
456, 521 A2d 811 (1987)
§§9.10, 11.10

Saunderlin v EI DuPont Co, 102
NJ 402, 508 A2d 1095 (1986)
§2.02

Search Warrant, In re, 810 F2d
67 (3d Cir 1987) §10.09

Seeglitz v State, 500 NE2d 144
(Ind 1986) §12.01

Sharpe v South Carolina Dept
of Mental Health, 354 SE2d
778 (SC Ct App 1987) §9.04

Simmons v State, 504 NE2d 575
(Ind 1987) §17.02

Simpson v Braider, 104 FRD
512 (DDC 1985) §10.02

Spencer v Industrial Commn,
733 P2d 158 (Utah 1987)
§14.10

Sprague v Bowen, 812 F2d
1226 (9th Cir 1987) §§14.16,
14.19

Stafford v Neurological
Medicine, Inc, 811 F2d 470
(8th Cir 1987) §14.03

State v Allewalt, 517 A2d 714
(Md 1986) §17.02

State v Anderson, 44 Wash App
644, 723 P2d 464 (1986)
§10.08

State v Bay, 150 Ariz 112, 722
P2d 280 (1986) §12.03

State v Black, 46 Wash App 259, 730 P2d 698 (1986) §§7.03, 17.02

State v Broadniak, 718 P2d 322 (Mont 1986) §17.02

State v Buell, 22 Ohio St 3d 124, 489 NE2d 795 (1986) §§17.01, 17.05

State v Champagne, 497 A2d 1242 (NH 1985) §11.06

State v Clements, 241 Kan 77, 734 P2d 1096 (1987) §13.10

State v Cooper, 708 SW2d 299 (Mo Ct App 1986) §17.01

State v Correll, 148 Ariz 468, 715 P2d 721 (1986) §11.10

State v DeLeonardo, 340 SE2d 350 (NC 1986) §13.10

State v Duell, 332 SE2d 246 (W Va 1986) §§6.19, 12.05

State v Eaton, 101 Nev 705, 710 P2d 1370 (1985) §14.04

State v Evans, 203 Conn 212, 523 A2d 1306 (1987) §12.03

State v Fishnick, 127 Wis 2d 247, 378 NW2d 272 (1985) §13.10

State v Fontaine, 382 NW2d 374 (ND 1986) §17.01

State v Friedrich, 135 Wis 2d 1, 398 NW2d 763 (1987) §13.10

State v Friend, 385 NW2d 313 (Minn Ct App 1986) §10.10

State v Gambrell, 318 NC 249, 347 SE2d 390 (1986) §12.03

State v Geyman, 729 P2d 475 (Mont 1986) §13.10

State v Halstead, 362 NW2d 504 (Iowa 1985) §17.01

State v Hiatt, 33 Or 60, 733 P2d 1373 (1987) §§13.10, 17.03

State v Hicks, 240 Kan 302, 729 P2d 1146 (1986) §17.03

State v Hodges, 239 Kan 63, 716 P2d 563 (1986) §§7.03, 12.01

State v Hudson, 152 Ariz 121, 730 P2d 830 (1987) §§11.10, 12.04

State v Huntley, 302 Or 418, 730 P2d 1234 (1986) §§2.02, 12.13

State v Irish, 391 NW2d 137 (Neb 1986) §10.02

State v Jackman, 396 NW2d 24 (Minn 1986) §12.01

State v Jackson, 239 Kan 463, 721 P2d 232 (1986) §13.10

State v Johnson, 714 So 2d 753, 758 (Mo Ct App 1986) §17.03

State v Johnson, 317 NC 343, 346 SE2d 596 (1986) §12.01

State v Johnson, 133 Wis 2d 207, 395 NW2d 176 (1986) §11.09

State v Kemp, 199 Conn 473, 507 A2d 1387 (1986) §17.01

State v Kim, 318 NC 614, 350 SE2d 347 (1986) §§13.10, 17.01

State v Lindsey, 149 Ariz 472, 720 P2d 72 (1986) §13.10

State v Logue, 372 NW2d 151 (ND 1985) §13.10

State v McQuillen, 239 Kan 590, 721 P2d 740 (1986) §17.02

State v Mercier, 128 NH 57, 509 A2d 1246 (1986) §§12.12, 16.04

State v Meyers, 359 NW2d 604 (Minn 1984) §13.10

Statutes

United States Code

28 USC §991 *et seq* **§12.09**

State Statutes

Cal Penal Code §29 (West Supp 1985) **§§9.08, 12.06**

Md Health-Gen §12-108 (Supp 1986) **§12.02**

Mo Stat Ann §475.075(1) (Vernon 1987) **§15.04**

NY Penal Law §40.15 (McKinney Supp 1987) **§12.02**

Tex Penal Code §8.01 (Vernon Supp 1987) **§12.02**

Tex R Crim Evid 509 **§10.04**

Rules and Regulations

Code of Federal Regulations

20 CFR 404, subpt P, app 1 §14.15

20 CFR 404, subpt P, app 61 §2.02

Federal Rules of Criminal Procedure

Fed R Crim P 12.2 §6.19

Federal Rules of Evidence

Fed R Evid 703 §9.05

Fed R Evid 704(b) §§9.08, 12.06

Fed R Evid 705 §9.05

Fed R Evid 803(4) §§9.03, 13.10